Statement Macramé For Beginners

Many Easy Patterns With Step By Step Tutorials

Copyright © 2020

All rights reserved.

DEDICATION

The author and publisher have provided this e-book to you for your personal use only. You may not make this e-book publicly available in any way. Copyright infringement is against the law. If you believe the copy of this e-book you are reading infringes on the author's copyright, please notify the publisher at: https://us.macmillan.com/piracy

Contents

DIY Macrame Wall Hanging 1

Make a Macrame Mason Jar Plant Hanger 15

Macrame Laptop Mat 25

DIY Macrame Feathers 32

Make a Scandinavian style knotted trivet 59

DIY Macrame Wall Hanging

A macrame wall hanging is an easy DIY project that will add a handmade touch to any room in your home. This free tutorial will help you create a wall hanging with a lot of interesting patterns, such as spirals and triangles. Don't be afraid to change it up to make it your own.

Despite how it looks, this is a simple project that will just take you an hour or two to complete. It really comes together fast and you'll find lots of opportunities to add your own style to it.

This is just one of many free macrame patterns that include plant hangers, bookmarks, curtains, and a whole lot more.

The knots you'll be using for this macrame wall hanging include Lark's Head knot, Spiral knot, and Square knot. You can learn how to tie all these knots by reading our guide on how to macrame.

What You'll Need

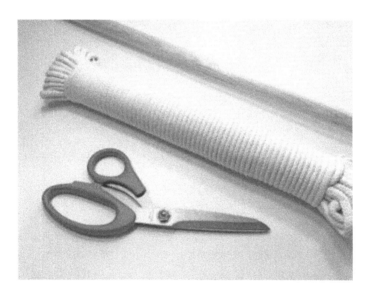

Here's what you'll need to complete this DIY macrame wall hanging:

Cotton Macrame Cord (200 feet or 61 meters)

Wooden Dowel (3/4-inch diameter, 24 inches long)

Scissors

I'm using cotton clothesline for my macrame cord. It has a wonderful natural look to it and is fairly inexpensive.

The wooden dowel doesn't need to be these exact dimensions and in place of the wooden dowel, use whatever size you like as long as you can fit all the ropes over it. If you'd like to give it a more outdoorsy feel, you could use a tree branch about the same size.

Make a Hanger for Your Wooden Dowel

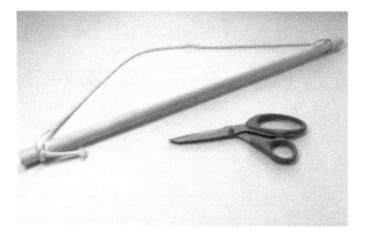

Cut a piece of macrame cord that's three feet (one meter). Tie each end of the cord to the two sides of the wooden dowel.

You'll use this to hang your macrame project when it's finished. I like to attach it at the beginning so I can hang the macrame project as I tie knots. Working this way is much easier than laying it down.

Cut Your Macrame Cord

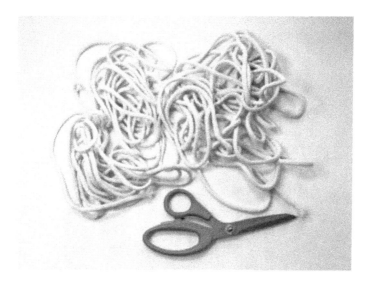

Cut your macrame cord into 12 lengths of rope that are 15 feet (4.5 meters) long.

This may seem like a lot of cord but knots take up more cord than you would think. There's no way to make your rope longer if you need to, so it's better to cut more than you'll use.

Attach Macrame Cord to Dowel

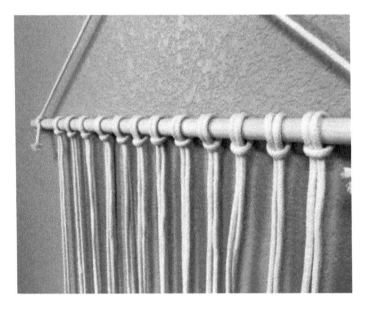

Fold one of the macrame cords in half and use a lark's head knot to attach it to the wooden dowel.

Attach all the other cords in the same way.

Knot Spiral Stitches

Take the first 4 cords and make a left-facing spiral stitch (also called a half knot sinnet) by tying 13 half knots.

Continue Knotting Spiral Stitches

Statement Macramé For Beginners

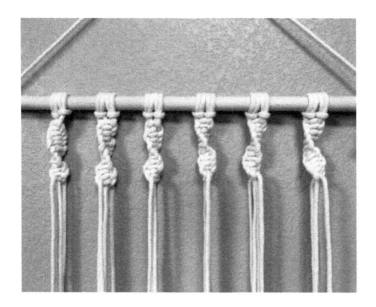

Use the next set of four ropes to make another spiral stitch with 13 half knots. Continue working in groups with four cords. When you finish, you should have a total of six spiral stitches.

Make Square Knots

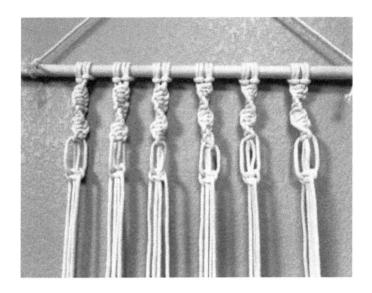

Measure approximately two inches down from the last knot in the spiral stitch. This is where you're going to place your next knot, the square knot.

Using the first four cords, make a right facing square knot. Continue making the right facing square knots all the way across this row. Do your best to keep them all horizontally even with each other. You'll end up with a set of six square knots.

Decrease Square Knots

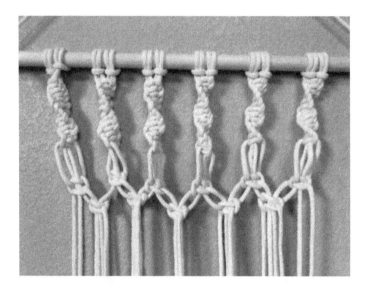

Now it's time to start decreasing the square knots so we can have a "V" shape of knots.

Leave the first two cords and the last two cords free. Make right facing square knots with each group of four. You'll now have a second row with the two first and two last cords unknotted and five square knots.

It doesn't matter how you space these, just keep them even with each other for each row.

Continue Deceasing the Square Knots

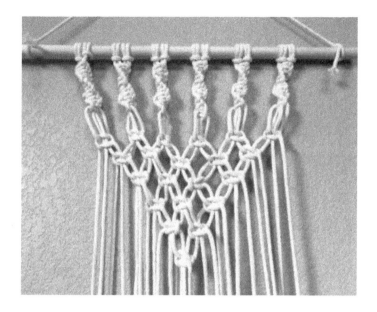

For the third row, you're going to leave out the first four cords and the last four cords. You'll have four square knots.

For the fourth row leave out six cords at the beginning and six cords at the end. You'll have three square knots.

In the fifth row, you'll leave out eight cords at the beginning and eight more cords at the end. You'll have two square knots now.

For the sixth and final row, you'll leave out 10 cords at the beginning and 10 cords at the end. This will leave you with four cords to make one final square knot.

Increase Square Knots

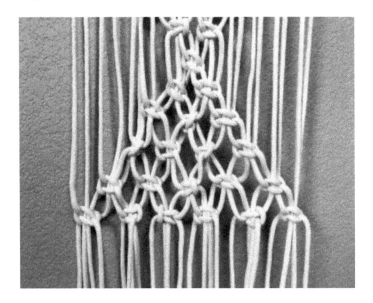

Time for more square knots! This time, we are going to be increasing them to form a triangle, or an upside down "V."

For the first row of this section, leave out the first eight and last eight cords. You'll make two square knots.

In the third row, leave out six cords at the beginning and the end. You'll have three square knots in this row.

For the fourth row, leave out four cords at the beginning and four at the end. You'll have four square knots.

In the fifth row, leave out two cords at the beginning and the last two cords. Now you'll have five square knots in this row.

For the last row, use all the cords to make knots. You'll have six square knots for this row.

Trim and Knot

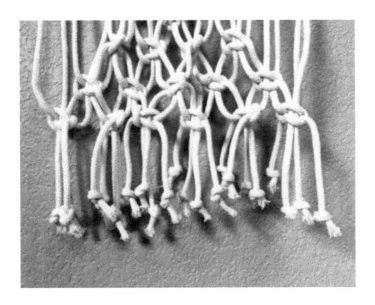

Time to give your macrame wall hanging a nice trim. Leave some space (about six to eight inches) under your final row. Use your scissors to cut the cords straight across.

You can leave it like how it is, add some beads, fray your ends, or tie simple overhand knots like above.

Make a Macrame Mason Jar Plant Hanger

Mason jars have stood the test of time when it comes to crafting supplies. From canning to organizing to hundreds of other creative uses, a mason jar will always come in handy.

With this macrame mason jar plant hanger, you can use any jar on hand to create a modern, clean, and very cool piece of decor for your home. These would look beautiful hanging in a group or hanging solo and would make the perfect housewarming gift for a new home or apartment. Create your macrame hanger as long or as short as you'd like and hang it in a sunny spot to keep your plant growing and healthy inside that mason jar.

What You'll Need

Mason jar

Macrame cord

Scissors

Soil

Plant

Gather Materials

For this project, you'll need a mason jar that's large enough to house a plant with a little room to grow. A pint-size or larger would most likely be a good place to start. For your macrame cord, choose your favorite type; they can vary from jute to cotton to polyester. It all depends on the look you like and the thickness you'd like your cord.

Cut and Knot

Cut four lengths of cord, each about three yards long. Fold them in half and knot them all together at the halfway point, leaving a loop at the knot. This will be where you hang your final project from the wall or ceiling.

Make Pairs

Separate the cords into pairs of two cords each. Leave about four to five inches from the top knot, and knot the pairs together.

Make Spiral Knots

Underneath each knotted pair, you'll now make a spiral knot pattern. Take one pair and hold the right cord taut. Cross the left cord over the right, around the back, and up through the loop it created. Pull tight. Keep repeating this process with the same cord, keeping the original right cord taut, and a spiral knot pattern will start to emerge. Repeat the spiral knots until you have about four inches of spiral knots.

Add Longer Knots

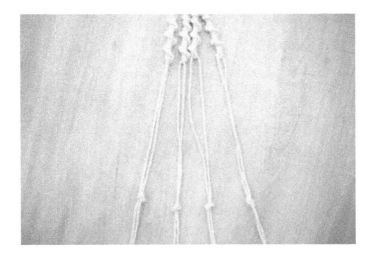

Once you have all of your pairs spiral knotted, leave a length of about 12 inches on each set of cords. At the 12 inch mark, make a knot with each pair of cords.

Alternate Pairs

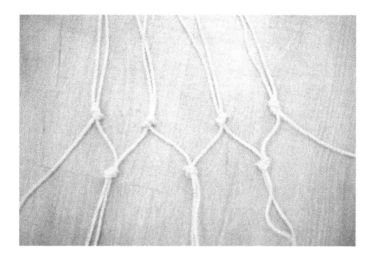

Lay all of your pairs out. From the leftmost pair, take the right cord and knot it with the left cord from the next closest pair, about three inches below the previous knot. Repeat the process, alternating pairs. At the end take the two outer cords and knot them together.

Knot Cords

About 3 inches below that set of knots knot all cords together in one large knot. Leave approximately 12 inches of hanging cord and trim the ends.

Plant Your Plant

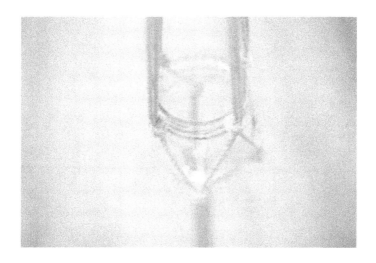

Insert your mason jar, and fill with soil and plants. Depending on the size of your greenery, it may be easier to plant it first and then fit your mason jar into the macrame hanger.

Hang and Enjoy

These mini planters are so cute, we don't see why you shouldn't make three or four and spruce up your office space, bedroom, or kitchen!

Macrame Laptop Mat

Yarns

144m[472.5ft] Phildar phil corde (100% cotton in off white)

Tools & Materials

Wooden board

4-5 clips

Scissors

Measuring tape

Size

25cm[9.8"] x45cm[17.7"]

Knots used

Square knot

Horizontal double half hitch

Diagonal double half hitch

Instructions

Begin

Measure and cut 48 pieces of 3m[9.8ft] yarn. Leaving approximately 10cm[3.9"] of yarn, secure the yarns to a wooden board using 4-5 clips to begin knotting.

Continue

1st row: Tie 12 square knots from left to right.

2nd row: Skip the first 2 strands. Create a square knot with 2 strands from the first square knot and 2 strands from the second square knot of the 1st row. Continue knotting 10 more square knots to have 11 square knots in a row.

3rd - 10th row: Make rows of square knots, skipping the first 2 strands for the 4th, 6th, 8th and 10th row.

11th row: Complete a row of horizontal double half hitch.

12th row: Skip 3 strands and knot the next 5 square knots.

13th row: Skip 5 strands and knot the next 4 square knots.

14th row: Skip 7 strands and knot the next 3 square knots.

15th row: Skip 9 strands and knot the next 2 square knots.

16th row: Skip 11 strands and knot the next 1 square knot.

Return to 12th row: Using the 3rd strand as the holding cord, tie 10 double half hitchfrom left to right diagonally down. Using the 24th strand as the holding cord, tie 10 double half hitch from right to left diagonally down. Skip the 25th strand and knot the next 5 square knots.

Return to 13th row: Skip the 25th -27th strand and knot the next 4 square knots.

Return to 14th row: Skip the 25th -29th strand and knot the next 3 square knots.

Return to 15th row: Skip the 25th -31st strand and knot the next 2 square knots.

Return to 16th row: Skip the 25th -33rd strand and knot the next 1 square knots.

Return to 12th row: Using the 25th strand as the holding cord, tie 10 double half hitchfrom left to right diagonally down. Using the 46th strand as the holding cord, tie 10 double half hitch from right to left diagonally down.

13th-21st row: Tie square knots to create a diamond pattern as shown in the diagram below.

Continue knotting the pattern with square knots and diagonal double half hitch until you get the pattern as shown below.

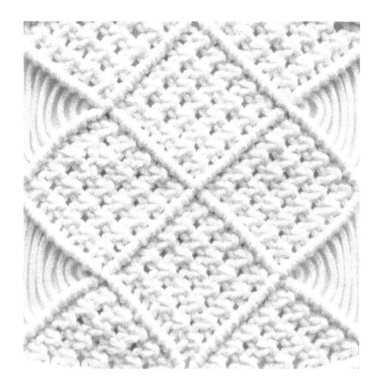

33rd row: Complete a row of horizontal double half hitch.

34th-43rd row: Make rows of square knots, skipping the first 2 strands for the 34th, 36th, 38th, 40th, 42nd row.

End

Cut off the both ends neat and even to lengths of your preference.

DIY Macrame Feathers

You'll Need:

5mm single twist cotton string

fabric stiffener

sharp fabric shears

cat brush

ruler

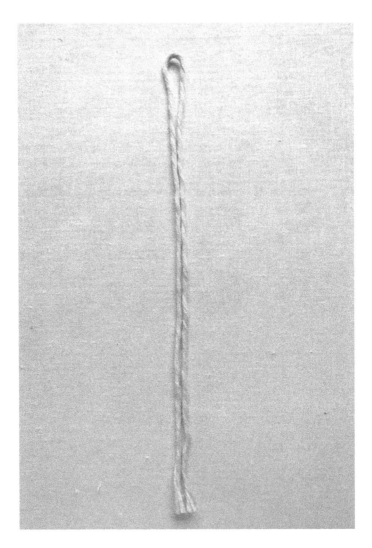

For a medium sized feather, cut:

Statement Macramé For Beginners

1 32" strand for the sprine

Statement Macramé For Beginners

10-12 14" strands for the top

8-10 12" strands for the middle

6-8 10" strands for the bottom

Fold the 32" strand in half.

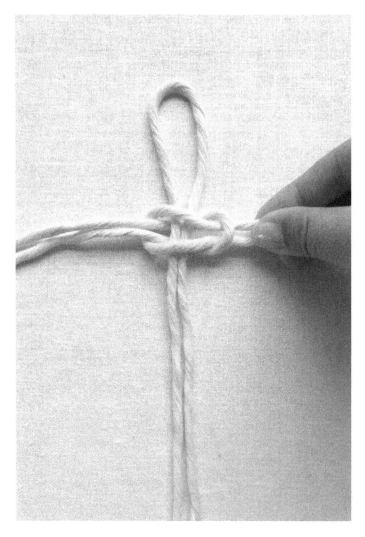

Take one of the 14" strands, fold it in half and tuck it under the spine.

Take another 14" strand, fold it in half and insert it into the loop of the top horizontal strand.

Statement Macramé For Beginners

Pull it through and lay it horizontally, on top of the opposing strand.

Now pull the bottom strands all the way through the top loop.

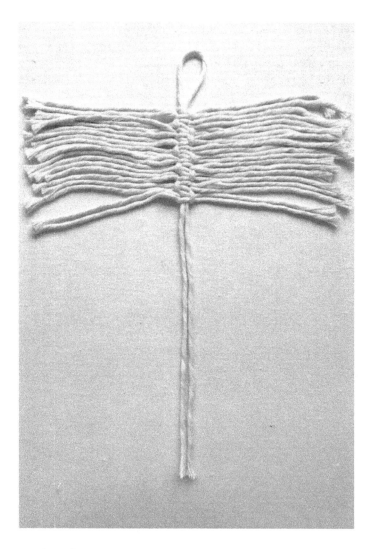

This is your knot!

Pull both sides tightly.

On the next row, you'll alternate the starting side. So if you laid the horizontal strand from left to right the first time, you'll lay the horizontal strand from right to left next.

Lay the first folded strand under the spine, thread another folded strand into its loop. Pull the lower strands through the top loop. And tighten.

Keep going and work gradually down in size.

Be sure to push the strands up to tighten - grab the bottom of the middle (spine) strand with one hand and with another, push the strands up. Once you're done, drag the fringe downwards to meet the bottom of the middle strand.

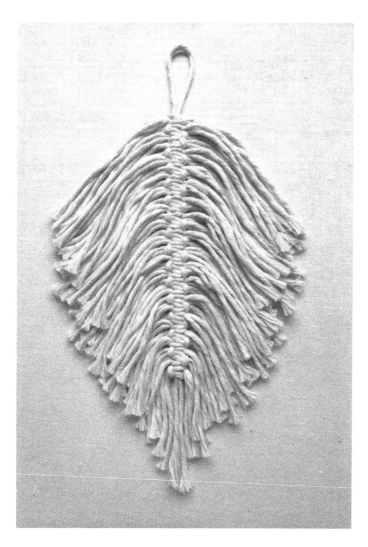

Then, give it a rough trim.

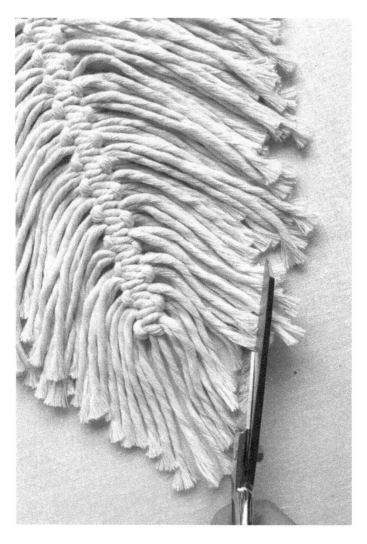

This not only helps guide the shape but also helps with brushing the strands out. The shorter the strands, the easier, to be honest. It also helps to have a very sharp pair of fabric shears!

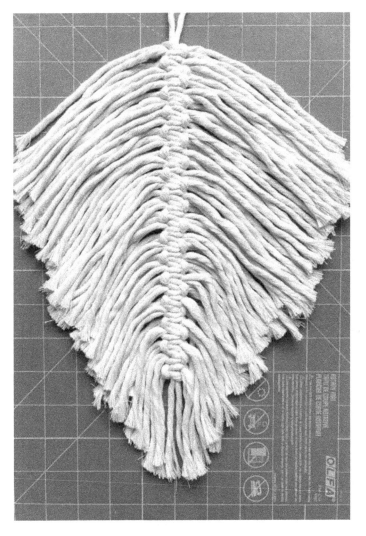

After a rough trim, place the feather on a durable surface as you'll be using an animal brush to brush out the cording.

The brush will damage any delicate or wood surface so I suggest using a self healing cutting mat or even a flattened cardboard box.

When brushing, start at the spine and push hard into the cording when brushing.

It'll take several hard strokes to get that beautiful, soft fringe.

Work your way down. When you're at the bottom, hold the bottom of the spine while brushing - you don't want the brush to yank any strands off!

Next, you'll want to stiffen the feather. The cording is so soft that it'll just flop if you pick it up and try to hang it. Give it spray, or two, and allow to try for at least a couple of hours.

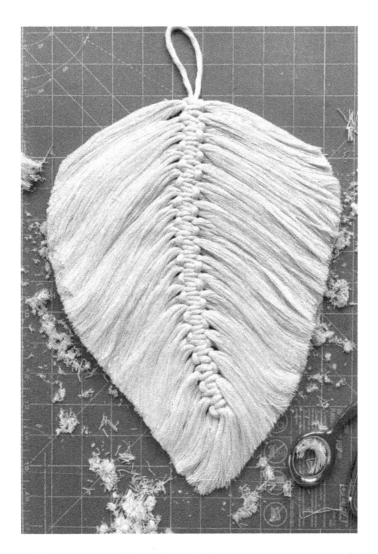

Once your feather has stiffened up a bit, you can now go back and give it a final trim. This, I would say, is the most challenging part. Take it easy. It's better to trim less than more! And you might need to adjust your trim depending on how often you're moving the piece. Once you're done trimming, you can even give it another stray of fabric stiffener for good measure. And then, you'll be ready to hang your piece!

Make a Scandinavian style knotted trivet

Think of Scandinavian design and the words minimal, simple and natural might come to mind. Minimal and simple design and colour palettes. Natural materials and tones. I designed this knotted macrame trivet tutorial with that Scandi design aesthetic in mind.

I made two trivets which can be used individually, or they can nest inside one another. I only used two very simple macrame knots, so this is something easy that you can make for your home or for a gift.

MATERIALS

You'll need a wooden embroidery hoop (I used one 5 inch and one 7 inch hoop), some wooden beads, and cotton rope (mine is 4mm cotton sash cord).

You may be surprised at the amount of rope you'll need – I was! The 5 inch embroidery hoop has a circumference of 46 cm (18 inches) and I used 6.4 metres (21 feet) of rope. So the amount of rope I used is almost 14 x the circumference.

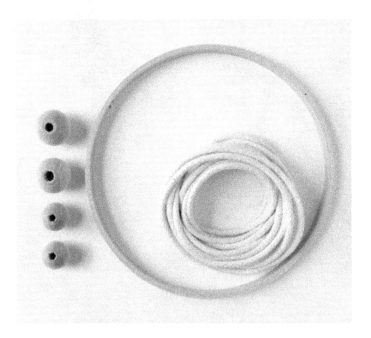

LET'S GET STARTED

We will be working with two pieces of rope at the same time – for the 5 inch trivet that means two lengths measuring 320 cm each. Wind the bulk of the cord up to make it more manageable and secure it with a rubber band.

First image below (top left): Leaving a tail of about 20 cm hold the rope and the hoop with one hand. Pass the rope over the hoop, down through the centre of the hoop, back up the front of the hoop and through the loop you just created.

While still holding the rope in place with one hand tighten the knot, making sure the two lengths of rope are parallel to each other and don't become twisted.

Repeat this knot around the circumference of the hoop. So pass the rope back down through the centre of the hoop, underneath the hoop and back up the front. Then through the loop. Make sure the two ropes are parallel to each other and tighten the knot. Easy.

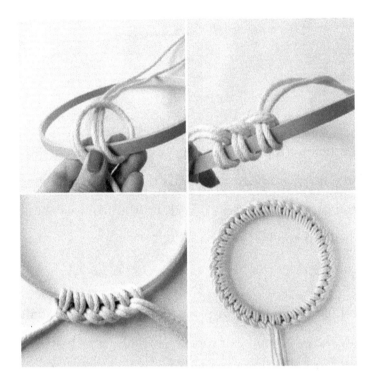

To finish join the four tails together with a square knot. Straighten the four tails and lay them parallel to each other.

First image below (top left): Take rope number 4, pass it over the two centre ropes and under rope 1.

Second image below (top right): Take rope number 1, pass it under the two centre ropes and up through the loop created by rope 4. Pull the knot tight.

Third image below (bottom left): Take rope number 1, pass it over the two centre ropes and under rope 4.

Fourth image below (bottom right): Take rope number 4, pass it under the two centre ropes and up through the loop created by rope 1. Pull the knot tight.

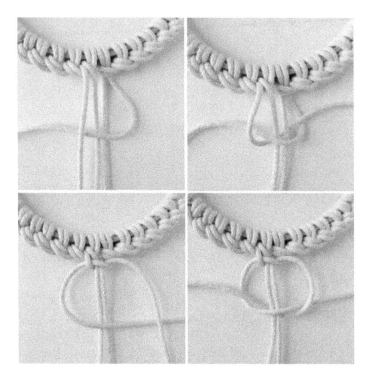

Add a bead to each of the four rope tails, and tie an overhand knot under the beads. Cut the extra length of the tails off so the beads are placed randomly. Fray the ends of the ropes.

If you'd like the trivets to nest inside each other the smaller one should be made without beads. Simply trim the tails to about 10 cm (4 inches) long, tie a single knot and tuck the ends under the trivet. Secure them with a hot glue gun.

Statement Macramé For Beginners

CPSIA information can be obtained
at www.ICGtesting.com
Printed in the USA
LVHW032116110223
739283LV00005B/147